HUMAN BODY

Troll Associates

HUMAN BODY

by Francene Sabin

Illustrated by Don Sibley

Troll Associates

Library of Congress Cataloging in Publication Data

Sabin, Francene.
    Human body.

    Summary: Describes the most complex machine in the
world and explains how it works.
    1. Body, Human—Juvenile literature. [1. Body,
Human. 2. Anatomy, Human. 3. Human physiology]
I. Sibley, Don, ill.   II. Title.
QP37.S23   1984   612   84-2591
ISBN 0-8167-0170-9 (lib. bdg.)
ISBN 0-8167-0171-7 (pbk.)

The human body is the most wonderful, complex machine in the world. Your body can walk and run, climb and sit. It can see, hear, smell, taste, and feel. It can eat, talk, laugh, lift things, play games, think, and read.

While these things are going on, you are breathing; there is blood flowing through your blood vessels; you are digesting food; and your body is doing a million other jobs at the same time! All through your life this marvelous machine is at work—even when you are sleeping.

Each one of us—inside and outside and from top to bottom—is made of billions of cells too small to be seen without a microscope. There are bone cells and fat cells, nerve cells and muscle cells, and many other kinds of cells.

Each kind of cell is part of a special team with a special job to do. A group of cells, all of the same kind, is called a tissue. The tissue that forms the outer layer of the human body is called the epidermis, or outer skin. In a way, you live inside a smooth, waterproof container. That soft-yet-tough container is your skin.

Your skin keeps your blood and other body fluids inside. It protects you from harmful bacteria, from the sun's rays, and from dirt. Your skin helps to keep your body's inside temperature from getting too hot or too cold. It has nerves in it that carry information to your brain. And the best thing about your skin is how well it fits you. It bends and stretches, then springs back to shape. And if you get a scratch or a cut or a scrape, your skin will mend itself.

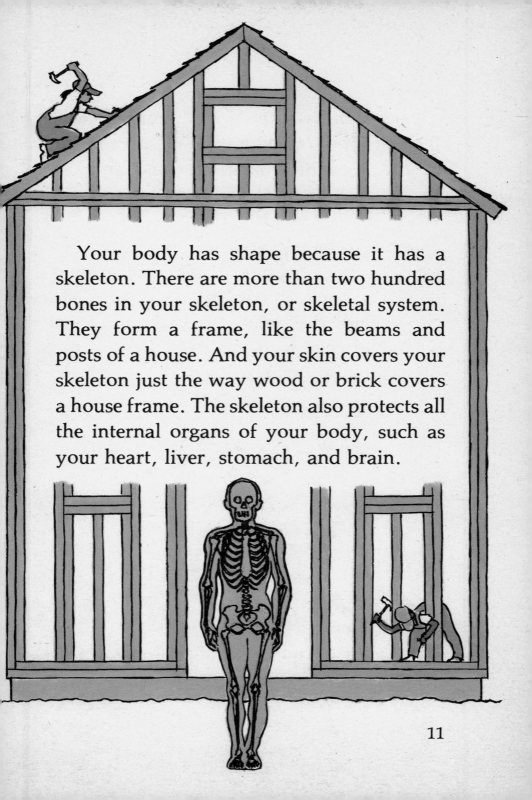

Your body has shape because it has a skeleton. There are more than two hundred bones in your skeleton, or skeletal system. They form a frame, like the beams and posts of a house. And your skin covers your skeleton just the way wood or brick covers a house frame. The skeleton also protects all the internal organs of your body, such as your heart, liver, stomach, and brain.

Your skull is at the top of your skeleton. It covers your brain and gives shape to your head. It is connected to your spine, or back-bone—a column of hollow bones called vertebrae.

Also attached to your backbone are your ribs—twenty-four bones that curve around from the back of your body towards the front. These ribs, twelve on each side, form a kind of cage for your heart, lungs, and other internal organs.

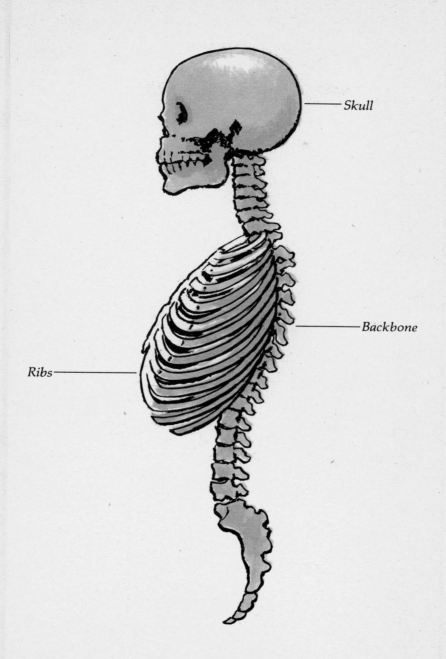

Skull

Backbone

Ribs

13

The bones that form your shoulders are fastened to your spinal column near the base of your neck. Connected to your shoulders are your arm bones. And of course, at the other end of your arm bones are the bones of your hands.

At the bottom of your spinal column are the flat bones that form the pelvic girdle. The pelvic girdle protects internal organs, such as your intestines, in which food is digested.

Connected to the pelvic bones are the leg bones. At the other end of the leg bones are the foot bones.

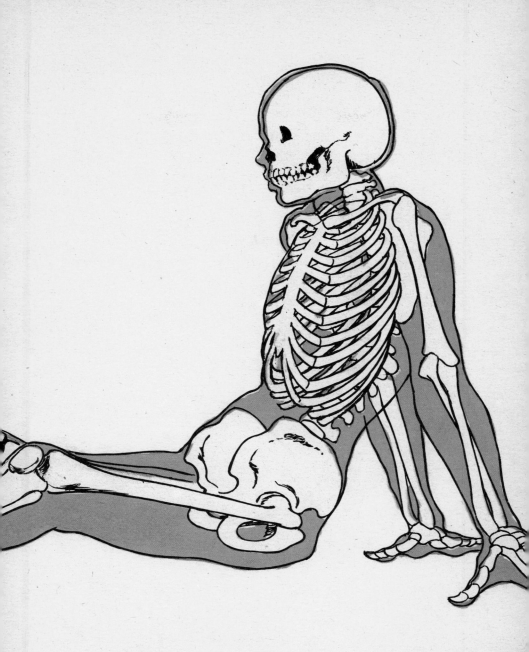

The place where two bones meet is called a joint. Some joints do not move, but most do. That's why you can bend, walk, and pick up things.

To keep the bones from rubbing against each other at the joints, there is a tough, springy tissue called cartilage. Cartilage cushions the jolts of movement.

Knee joint

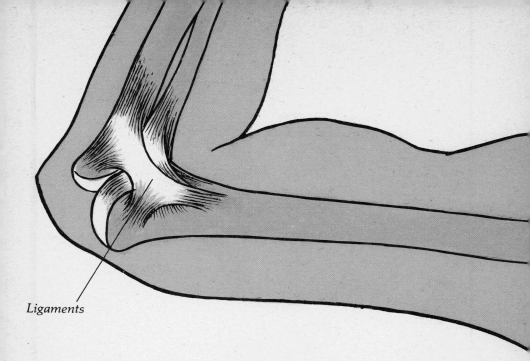

Ligaments

Your bones are held together at the joints by tissue called ligaments. The ligaments are like cords that stretch as the joint moves, but grip the bones firmly so they will not part.

Bones are hard on the outside, soft and spongy inside. The hard, white outside is made of calcium and other minerals. The soft inside, called marrow, is either red or yellow. Yellow marrow is made up mostly of fat cells. Red bone marrow is where red blood cells are made.

Muscles and tendons

Your muscles move the bones of your skeletal system. Muscles are bunches of strong tissue. Often they are connected to bones by cords called tendons. When you want to move, you use *voluntary* muscles. Voluntary muscles are under your control.

There are also *involuntary* muscles, which you do not control. They work automatically. Your heart is an involuntary muscle that pumps blood through your body. The muscles that open and close the pupils of your eyes are involuntary muscles.

It takes energy for all the muscles of your body to work. This energy comes from the food you eat, which is processed by the digestive system.

Digestion begins in your mouth. First, you take in food, biting it into small pieces with your front teeth and grinding it up with your other teeth. When the food is small enough to swallow easily, it goes from your mouth through your esophagus and into your stomach. Then it continues through your small and large intestines.

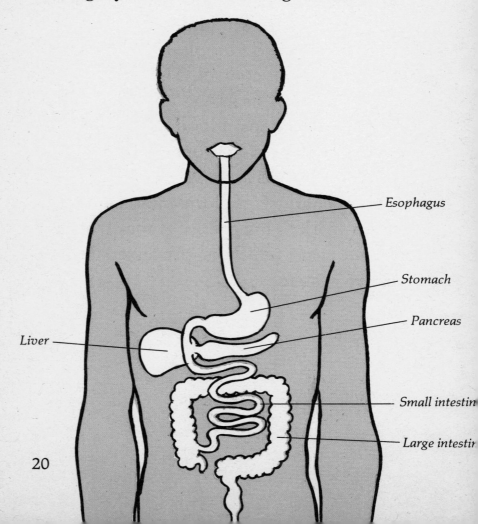

Esophagus

Stomach

Pancreas

Liver

Small intestin

Large intestin

20

All of these organs together make up a kind of long tube called the alimentary canal. The digestive system is made up of the alimentary canal, the liver, the pancreas, and other organs.

The food you eat contains vitamins, minerals, starch, fats, and proteins. But you cannot use these elements to build bone and blood and muscle until they have been digested. Digestion is the process of breaking down foods into nutrients that your body can use. These foods are broken down by chemicals called enzymes.

Once the food is changed into nutrients, the nutrients are carried to every part of your body by your circulatory system. Your circulatory system is like a delivery service. It runs throughout every part of your body, carrying to your cells everything they need, and carrying away what they don't need.

Your circulatory system is made up of your heart, arteries, veins, and very thin blood vessels called capillaries. If all your blood vessels were laid end to end, they would reach around the world—*four times!*

Each time your heart beats, it pumps blood through your arteries. Your blood is made up of red blood cells carrying oxygen, white blood cells that fight disease, platelets that help the blood to clot, and a liquid called plasma. After your body takes what it needs and gives back what it does not need, the blood makes a return trip through your veins. So arteries lead away from your heart, and veins lead back.

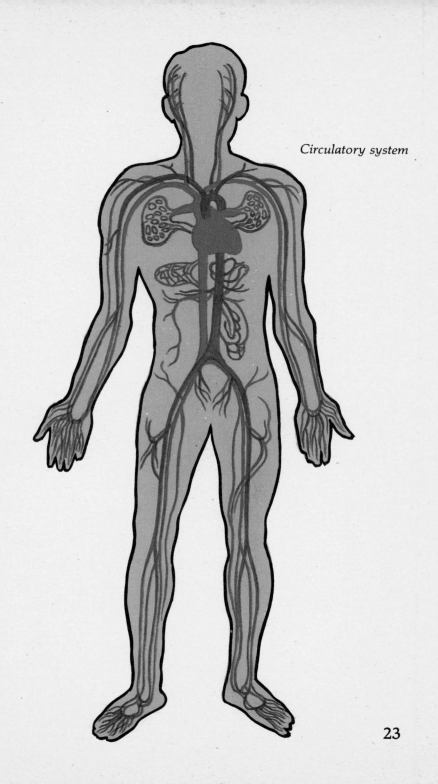

Circulatory system

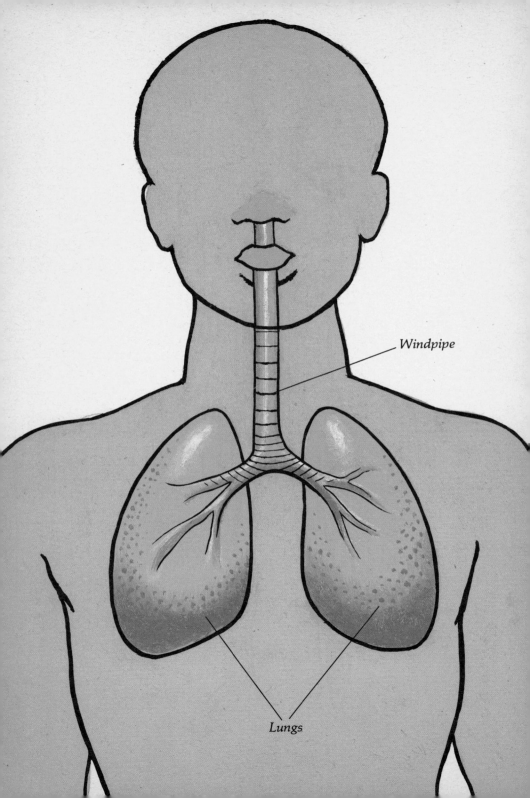

Windpipe

Lungs

Your body needs oxygen to change nutrients into energy. Oxygen enters your body in the air you breathe. Air comes in through your nose or mouth, moves down your windpipe and into your lungs.

Your lungs are the most important part of your respiratory system, or breathing system. You have two lungs, made up of millions of tiny air pouches. The walls of these air pouches are lined with tiny blood vessels. There, oxygen passes from the air pouches into your bloodstream. And carbon dioxide wastes pass from your bloodstream into your lungs, so they can be breathed out.

Breathing, like digestion and the circulation of blood, is controlled by nerve messages from your brain. Your brain is like a super computer that controls the machinery of your body.

Part of your brain called the medulla regulates the involuntary muscles of your body. Other parts of your brain do other jobs. The cerebrum controls conscious, or voluntary, activities. When you read and understand, remember, and solve problems, you are using the cerebrum. Physical activities, such as walking, dancing, and swimming, are controlled by the cerebellum.

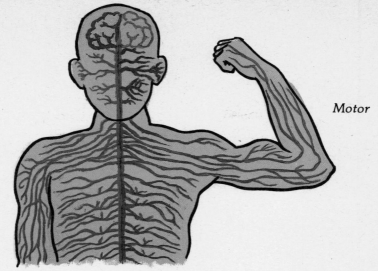

Motor

Sensory

Messages from all parts of your brain travel through your body along a network of nerve cells. Your brain, your spinal cord, and the many millions of nerve cells in your body make up your nervous system. The messages themselves are weak electrical impulses. You have two kinds of nerves. Motor nerves carry messages from your brain to your muscles. Sensory nerves carry messages to your brain from your sense organs.

Your sense organs tell you everything about the world around you. Ears hear; eyes see; taste buds taste; your nose smells; and your skin feels. These are your outer sense organs. Your inner sense organs feel such things as hunger, thirst, and pain.

Every human being's body contains many other organs that do important jobs. There is a reproductive system that makes it possible for the human race to go on. There is a lymphatic system, made up of lymph glands and vessels, that helps the white blood cells fight disease. And there is an endocrine system, made up of important glands that produce hormones.

Hormones are chemical substances that regulate many of the body's functions. The thyroid gland makes the hormone thyroxin, which controls how fast the cells use up nutrients. In this way, thyroxin controls growth and energy.

The pituitary gland makes many hormones. One of its hormones controls growth during childhood. So your pituitary gland determines how tall you will be. There are also hormones that affect your heartbeat, your breathing, and your feelings.

Your body is a very complex machine. It contains millions and millions of cells that form tissues. The tissues form organs. And the organs work together to form complicated systems. The systems give your body shape and help it to move and keep it working—day and night, year after year.

But you only have one body, so take care of it. It really is a remarkable piece of machinery. In fact, it's the most wonderful machine in the entire world.